Animal Classifications

Invertebrates

Angela Royston

heinemann
raintree

Edited by Helen Cox Cannons, Clare Lewis, and
    Abby Colich
Designed by Steve Mead
Picture research by Tracy Cummins
Production by Victoria Fitzgerald
Originated by Capstone Global Library Ltd
Printed and bound in China by Leo Paper Group

18 17 16 15 14
10 9 8 7 6 5 4 3 2 1

Library of Congress Cataloging-in-Publication Data
Royston, Angela, 1945- author.
    Invertebrates / Angela Royston.
        pages cm—(Animal classification)
    Summary: "This fascinating series takes a very simple
look at animal classifications, with each book focusing on a
different group of animal. This book is about invertebrates:
what they do, how they behave, and how these
characteristics are different from other groups of animals.
Beautifully illustrated with colorful photographs, the book
shows many examples of different types of invertebrates in
their natural environment."—Provided by publisher.
    Includes bibliographical references and index.
    ISBN 978-1-4846-0752-7 (hb)—ISBN 978-1-4846-0759-6
(pb)—ISBN 978-1-4846-0796-1 (ebook) 1. Invertebrates—
Juvenile literature. 2. Animals—Classification—Juvenile
literature. I. Title.

QL362.4.R69 2015
592—dc23   2014013459

**This book has been officially leveled by using the F&P
Text Level Gradient™ Leveling System.**

Acknowledgments
We would like to thank the following for permission to
reproduce photographs: iStockphotos: AtWaG, 6; Science
Source: D.P. Wilson / FLPA, 23; Shutterstock: Bennyartist,
10, Bonnie Taylor Barry, 13, Borisoff, 27, Denis Vesely, 12, 29
Top, EcoPrint, 11, 29 Bottom, Edwin van Wier, 4, Fotochip,
17, Igor Gorelchenkov, Cover, ILeysen, 25, Klagyivik Viktor,
16, Litvintsev Ihor, 7, Marinerock, 14,
Mauro Rodrigues, 19, 29 Middle, MaZiKab, 21, Melola,
15, Mirvav, 18, ninii, 5, Protasov AN, Design Element,
RazvanZinica, 20, Rich Carey, 8, val lawless, 24, Vlad61, 26,
yevgeniy11, 22, 28; SuperStock: Dave Fleetham / Pacific
Stock - Design Pics, 9.

We would like to thank Michael Bright for his invaluable
help in the preparation of this book.

Contents

Some words are shown in bold, **like this**. You can find out what they mean by looking in the glossary.

Meet the Invertebrates

Scientists divide living things into groups. This is called **classification**. A starfish and a ladybug do not look much alike, but they belong to the same huge group of animals. This group is called the **invertebrates**. Invertebrates do not have a backbone inside their bodies.

A starfish lives at the bottom of the sea.

A ladybug is an insect with wings and six legs.

Invertebrates are **classified** into many smaller groups, such as insects. Each group is different from other groups in particular ways.

Animals with Shells

Some **invertebrates** have soft bodies. They are called **mollusks**. Some mollusks build a strong shell around their bodies. The shell protects the animal's body and gives it its shape. Limpets, mussels, and oysters are all mollusks that live in water.

Mussels and limpets cling to rocks.

mussel

limpet

eyes

foot

A snail has two eyes, one at the end of each eyestalk.

A snail is a mollusk too. A snail carries its shell on its back as it moves along. If it is scared, it pulls its head and its one large foot back into the shell.

Squids and Octopuses

Squids and octopuses are **mollusks,** even though they do not have a shell! Some squids are very large. They have eight arms and two **tentacles.** Giant squids grow up to 59 feet (18 meters) long.

A squid uses its two tentacles to catch food.

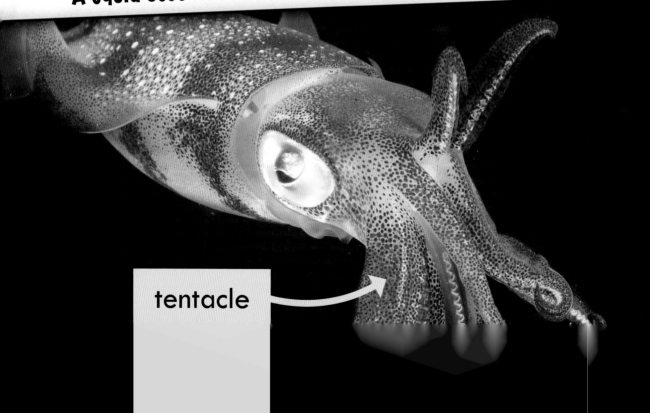

tentacle

suction pad

An octopus has suction pads along its arms.
It uses them to grasp food and rocks.

Octopuses and squids can move fast
by using their bodies like a **jet engine**.
For example, an octopus pushes water
backward out of its body so that it can
shoot forward!

Crabs, Lobsters, and Shrimps

Crabs, lobsters, and shrimps belong to a group of **invertebrates** called **crustaceans**. Their bodies are covered by a hard **skeleton**, like a suit of armor.

Almost every part of a shrimp's body is protected by its skeleton.

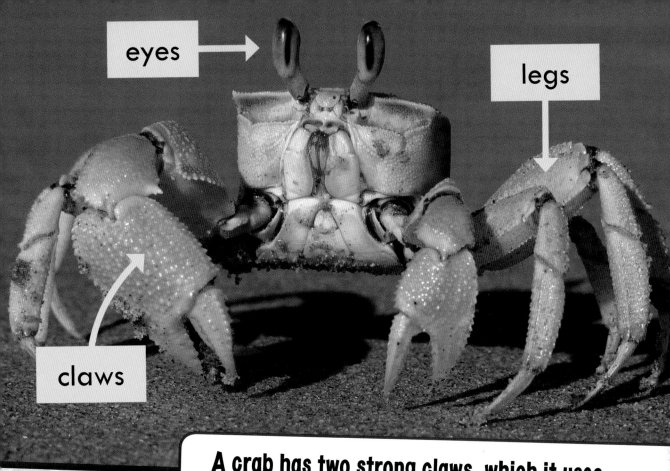

eyes

legs

claws

A crab has two strong claws, which it uses for fighting and for crushing food.

A crustacean's outer skeleton is made up of many parts, which fit together at the **joints**. Even a crustacean's long legs are protected by its skeleton. Some crabs walk sideways, because that is how their legs bend!

Insects

The largest group of **invertebrates** is insects. They include dragonflies, beetles, and grasshoppers. Like **crustaceans**, insects have a hard outer **skeleton**.

A grasshopper can fly, but it can also jump using its long back legs.

antenna

head

abdomen

thorax

six legs

All insects have similar bodies.

All adult insects have six legs. Their bodies are divided into three parts: a head, thorax, and abdomen. Some insects have two pairs of wings, and some have one pair. Some insects have no wings at all.

From Caterpillar to Butterfly

Many young insects look very different from adult insects. A caterpillar is a young butterfly. When the caterpillar is fully grown, it changes. The change is called **metamorphosis.**

A caterpillar eats and grows. Its favorite food is the leaf it **hatched** on.

As it changes, the caterpillar fixes itself to a leaf and sheds its skin. Under the skin is a kind of shell called a **pupa**. Inside the pupa, the caterpillar slowly becomes a butterfly.

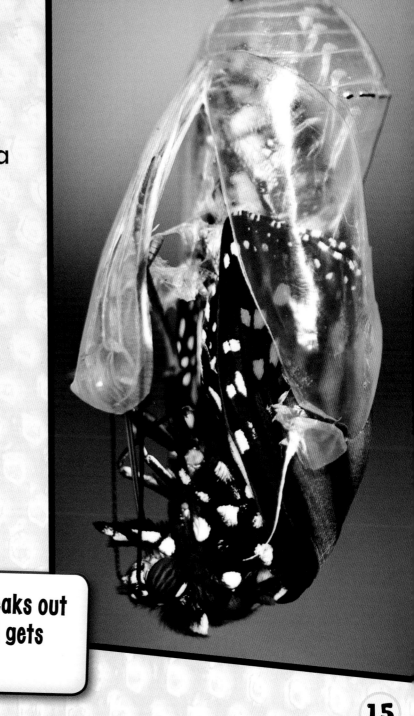

A butterfly breaks out of its pupa and gets ready to fly.

Living Together

Many insects live alone, but some live together in large groups. They include ants and some bees and wasps. The queen is the main insect in a group. For example, a queen honeybee sets up a nest with many worker bees.

Bees visit flowers to collect pollen and a sweet juice called nectar.

pollen

Bees make honey inside the nest.

The worker bees collect **pollen** and **nectar** from flowers. They feed the queen bee with nectar and store the pollen to make honey. Only the queen lays eggs, which **hatch** into new bees.

Spiders and Scorpions

It is easy to tell a spider from an insect. A spider has eight legs, a head, a body, and no wings. Most spiders feed on insects or other spiders.

Some spiders spin a web of silk thread to trap their **prey**.

head

body

web

A scorpion has a long tail, which it often curves over its back.

Scorpions have eight legs and belong to the same group as spiders. A scorpion has a **venomous** stinger at the end of its tail.

Many Legs

Centipedes have up to 354 legs, although most have about 30 legs. Centipedes live in the soil. They are fierce hunters and feed at night on insects and spiders.

A centipede can run as fast backward as it does forward.

A millipede curls up tight when it is in danger.

Millipedes have up to 750 legs—even more than centipedes. Millipedes also come out at night and feed mainly on rotting plants. Most millipedes live in the soil or among dead leaves on the ground.

Worms

Worms have no legs. Some worms live on the seashore. Others live in the soil. Earthworms feed on dead leaves and help to keep the soil healthy.

Earthworms swallow dead plants and turn them into soil.

Tube worms live around hot spots on the ocean bed.

Tube worms are some of the strangest
animals. They live on the ocean bed and
in the rotting bodies of dead whales.
Giant tube worms can grow up to
6 and a half feet (almost 2 meters) long.

Jellyfish

Jellyfish, sea anemones, and corals belong to the same group. They all have **tentacles** and a mouth in the middle of their soft, jelly-like body.

A sea anemone looks more like a plant than an animal.

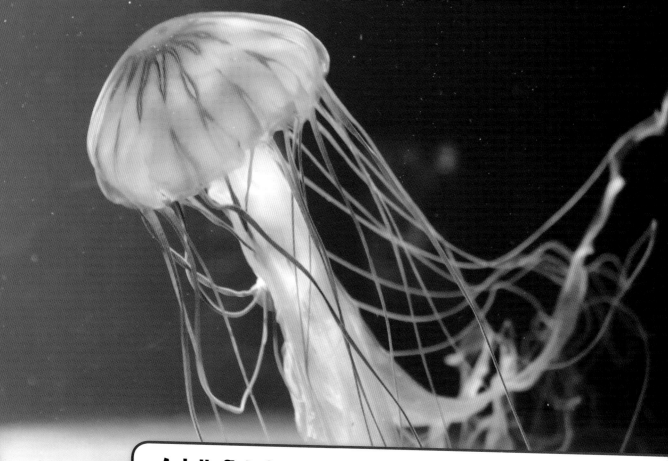

A jellyfish floats through the water. It uses its tentacles to defend itself and to catch **prey**.

Some jellyfish have very long tentacles, which can be 100 feet (30 meters) or longer. The tentacles contain **venomous** stingers. Some jellyfish are so venomous they can harm a person.

Incredible Coral

A coral reef is amazing. It is made by millions of tiny animals called **coral polyps**. The **skeletons** of polyps grow on top of old, empty skeletons. Over millions of years, the reef slowly gets bigger.

Coral reefs can be very colorful.

The Great Barrier Reef stretches 1,400 miles (2,300 kilometers) along the coast of Australia.

Coral reefs provide a home for many **invertebrates**. In fact, more types of sea animals live around coral reefs than anywhere else in the ocean.

Quiz

Look at the pictures below and read the clues. Can you remember the names of these **invertebrates**? Look back in the book if you need help.

1. I have no legs and live in the soil. What am I?

2. I have six legs and can jump as well as fly. What am I?

3. I have eight legs and a stinger in my tail. What am I?

4. I have a hard outer **skeleton** and two big claws. What am I?

Glossary

classification system that scientists use to divide living things into separate groups

classified put into a group according to special things shared by that group

coral polyp tiny animal whose skeleton helps to build a coral reef

crustacean member of a group of invertebrates whose bodies, including their legs and claws, are covered with a hard, chalky skeleton

hatch break out of an egg

invertebrate member of a very large group of animals that do not have bones inside their bodies. Invertebrates do not have a backbone.

jet engine powerful machine that moves an airplane or boat forward by pushing air out of the back of the engine

joint place where two bones or pieces of hard shell meet. Joints allow legs and other body parts to move.

metamorphosis complete change in body shape that insects go through when the young become adults

mollusk member of a group of invertebrates, most of whom have a single shell or a double shell that protects their body

nectar sweet juice found in flowers

pollen fine yellow dust made by flowers

prey animal that is hunted by another animal for food

pupa stage an insect goes through when it changes from a caterpillar to a butterfly or moth

skeleton hard frame inside or outside the body that gives an animal its shape

tentacles long arms that an invertebrate uses to feel, to move, or to hold things

venomous full of venom. Venom is poison that is injected by a stinger.

Find Out More

Books

Berger, Melvin and Gilda. *Butterflies and Caterpillars* (True or False).
New York: Scholastic, 2008.

Schuetz, Kari. *Insects* (Blastoff!: Animal Classes). Minneapolis:
Bellwether Media, 2013.

Veitch, Catherine. *Bug Babies* (Animal Babies). Chicago:
Heinemann Library, 2013.

Web sites

FactHound offers a safe, fun way to find internet sites
related to this book. All of the sites on FactHound have
been researched by our staff.

Here's all you do:
Visit www.facthound.com
Type in this code: 9781484607527

Index